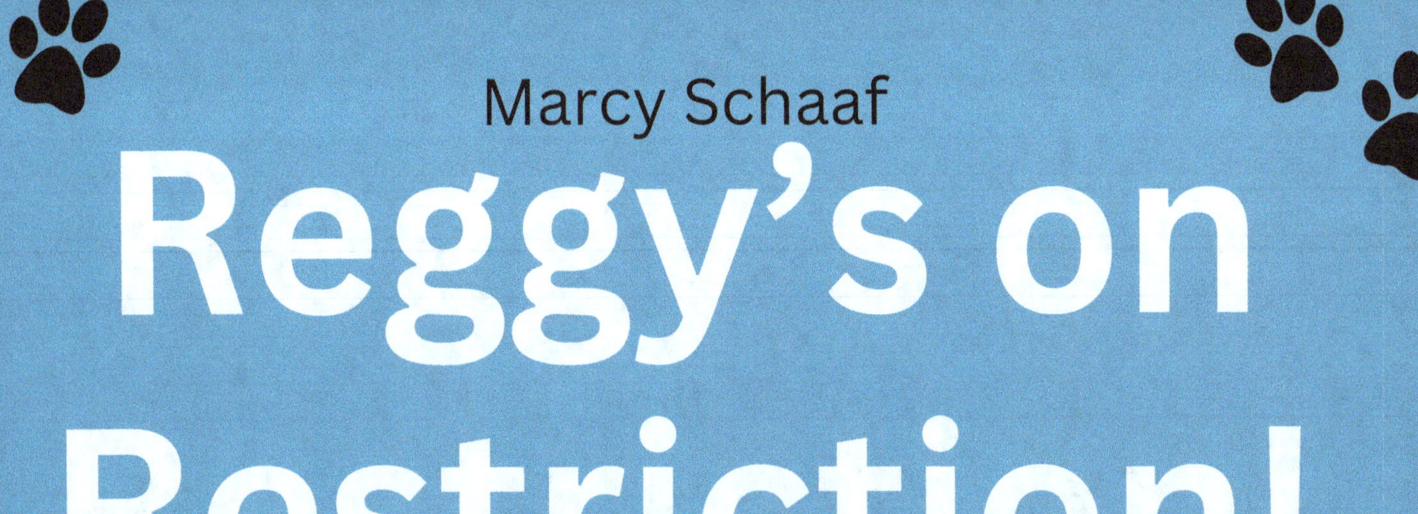

Marcy Schaaf
Reggy's on Restriction!
A Pawsitive Change.

∩F483882

English

Welcome to the heartwarming tale of "Reggy's On Restriction: A Pawsitive Change." In a cozy house, filled with laughter and wagging tails, there lived a mischievous dog named Reggy. But Reggy had a little problem - he was a bit of a bully. Join us as we embark on a journey with Reggy, exploring the ups and downs of his furry adventures. Discover how a special lesson and a touch of kindness transformed Reggy into the best doggy friend, making his house a joyful den. Get ready for a story that teaches the power of change, the magic of friendship, and the joy that comes from choosing kindness. Let's dive into Reggy's lesson and learn why being a little kinder can make our world a brighter place!

Once upon a time, in a cozy house, lived a mischievous dog named Reggy.

Reggy loved to bark, growl, and snatch toys from his furry friends.

His tail wagged with mischief, causing stress in the house each day.

Reggy's antics scared the little ones and made the house less fun.

Mom and Dad sighed,
wondering how to make
Reggy a good dog.

One day, they decided to put Reggy on a special doggy restriction.

Reggy couldn't chase, bark,
or be a bully for a while.

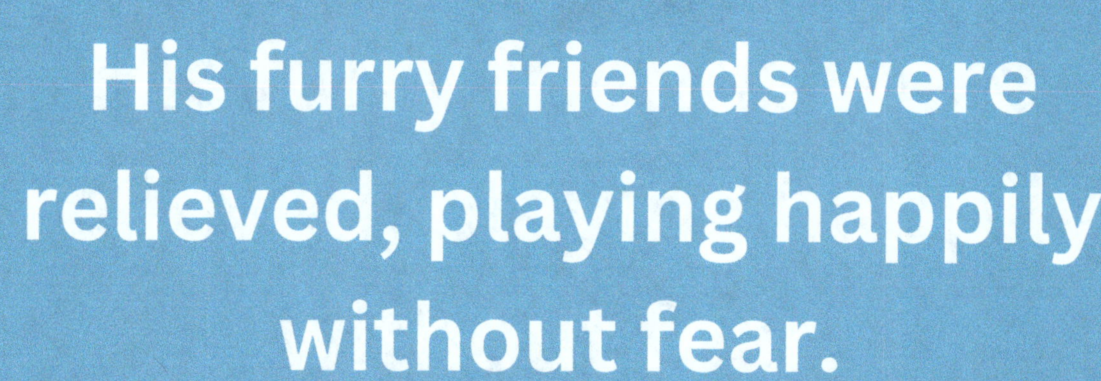

His furry friends were relieved, playing happily without fear.

Reggy felt sad with his restriction, wondering why things changed.

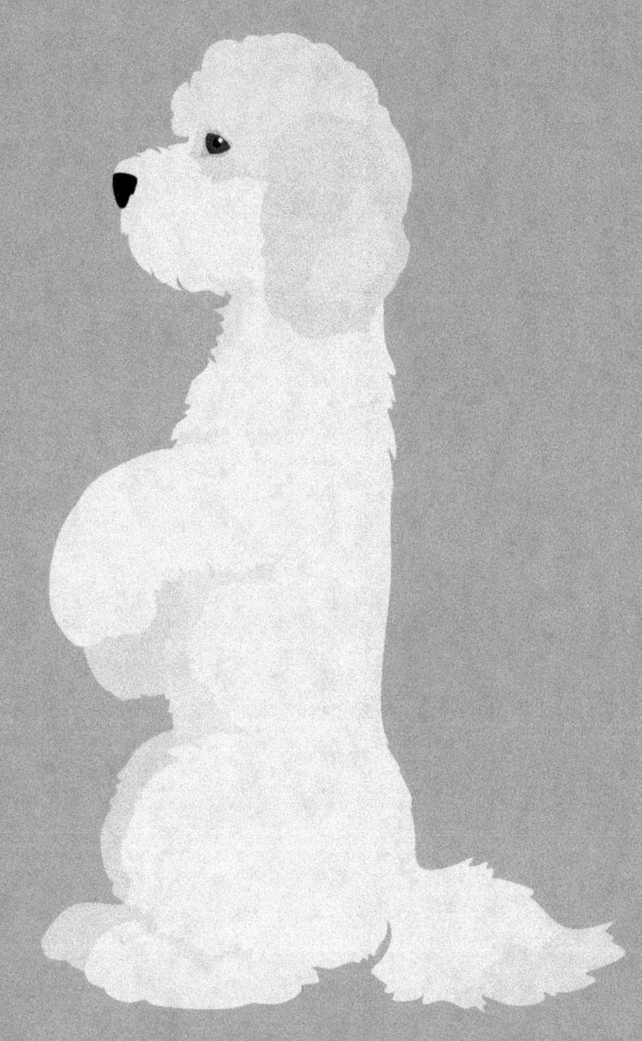

But soon, he discovered new ways to have fun without being mean.

He learned to share toys and play gently, making friends happy.

Reggy realized being kind brought joy and wagging tails all around.

Mom and Dad smiled, proud of the change in their furry friend.

The house became a happy place, full of laughter and wagging tails.

Reggy's friends forgave him, and they all played together again.

Reggy's heart swelled with happiness, grateful for the lesson learned.

Now, he was the best doggy friend, making the house a joyful den.

Reggy's story teaches us that kindness turns a frown upside down.

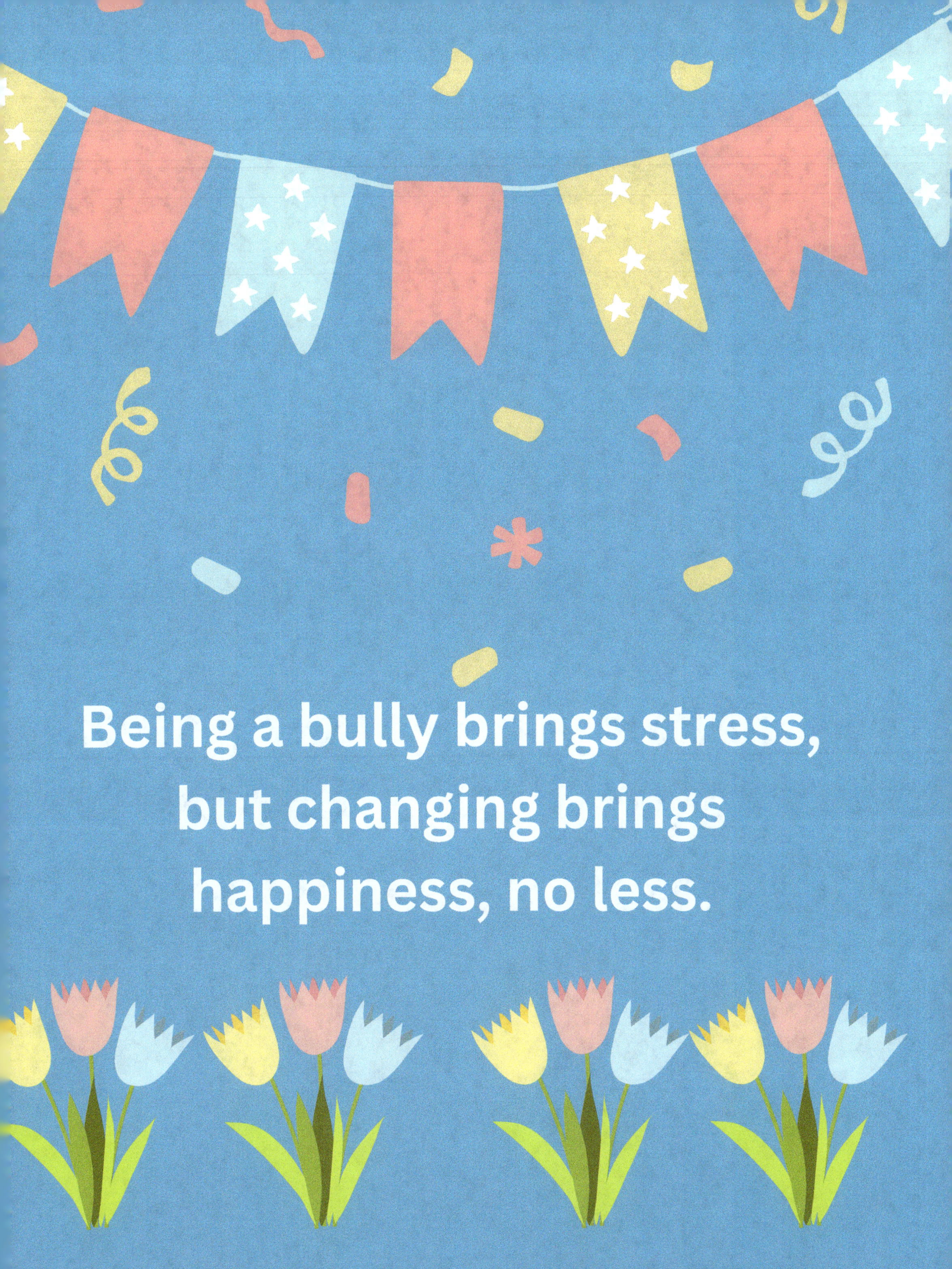

Being a bully brings stress,
but changing brings
happiness, no less.

So, let's remember the tale
of Reggy, the dog who
turned things around.

And be kind to our friends, making our homes a cheerful playground.

For kindness and love, with friends, is how joy is declared.

Now, in our hearts, let's
keep Reggy's story bright.

Be kind like Reggy, and
everything will be just right.

Remember the day when the house became stress-free.

Thanks to Reggy's change, a happy home it came to be.

Be like Reggy, choose kindness from the very start.

The end, sweet dreams, and may your world be full of love and cheer.

This book is about Reggy the real dog who was on restriction, who is now kind to his friends!

This story took place Italy

REMEMBER!

Be Kind

For more books like this visit:
www.BooksBySchaaf.com

Reggy's On Restriction is available in 10 languages

www.ingramcontent.com/pod-product-compliance
Lightning Source LLC
Chambersburg PA
CBHW081204130726
47996CB00009B/3238